HOW TO
BUY A CAR

Successfully Purchase Your Next Car!

DEVOE PELCHER

HOW TO BUY A CAR

ISBN-13:
978-1495339431

ISBN-10:
1495339432

Cover Design: GLORIA MARIE PELCHER

For all car buyers! Happy and safe driving!

CONTENTS

"The cars we drive say a lot about us."
Alexandra Paul

INTRODUCTION

This book is in a direct response to a friend that visited me over a Thanksgiving Holiday that lives in New York being very inquisitive about the car purchasing adventure. He was so hungry about retrieving information about buying a car, that he would come back and always ask or say "I was wondering could you tell me what the next part or the next phase in buying a car". So I would split the information over different phases as he returned through the holidays to receive more information on how to buy a car. He would get a little more every time.

Many people, like my friend, look for ways to save money and be resourceful when making purchases, especially when making a big purchase like a car. I have decided to produce this book because I have seen many people make mistakes when purchasing a car. Buying a car does not have to be an event filled with mistakes. Mistakes can be costly and very unbearable when making financial decisions. It matters not that you are an individual or a company with funds, if you are tired of going to the car dealership and feel like you are being cheated, being taken for everything that you have, and ending up leaving without what you really want, or what you went there to get, then this book is for you.

I will guide you through your next car buying experience. These tips are designed to make your car buying experience is pleasant. My ultimate goal is to minimize your losses. When you make your next decision to buy a car please remember these points when you do. I will cover how to best buy a car from a dealership, an individual, and tips for women buyers. I will also include and explain obtaining a vehicle through an auction.

1. BUYING A CAR FROM A DEALERSHIP

Before entering a car dealership you should be prepared. Know all the most significant numbers of the deal. For example, know the price of the car you are in the market for, the trade-in value of your current car (if you have one), and your desired monthly payments. Come to the dealership with a game plan, it could potentially be a knock-out drag down fight. At times it could feel like you are in a boxing ring.

Before you get to the car dealership

Know what you want when you go into the

dealership. It seems like this would be obvious, but if you haven't thought carefully about your needs you should really consider how you plan to use the car. How many people do you plan to carry? What about luggage? How often do you plan to use the car? Questions like these should be answered if you don't want to wind up as an unhappy car buyer.

Be honest with yourself. If you want a sunroof, place that on your list. Many people say they want safety, reliability, and mileage in their car, when in fact they're looking for performance, comfort, and appearance. Honestly will make the buying process much easier.

Go on the web and find the different options available for the type of car that you want to buy. The options that you want that are not there at the time may have to be placed on your vehicle at a later date, but make sure that you have them figured into the package before you get to the finance office.

Get the color that you want, even if they have to go to another dealer to pick it up and have it shipped to their dealership. They can do that for you, or you can go somewhere where the color that you want can be gotten for you. Don't be sucker punched into getting a color you do not want, this is an easy round to win.

Know your budget. A car salesperson's worst dream is an educated buyer: a buyer who knows what she or he wants, does not want to be impulsive, and is aware of what's available based on their budget and research. Stick to your budget even when the salesperson is attempting to impede upon your set budget.

Decide if you need a 4, 6, or 8 cylinder engine. Gas is not cheap so you don't want more car than you need. For example, If you do not have a large family there is no need to buy a large car that has 8 cylinders in it. Unless you are a performance type of person, then this does not apply to you. Also note, almost all of the large car models can be purchased in a 6 cylinder model.

Browse lot before going onto the sales floor. If you can, try to go to a dealership on a day/time when the dealership is closed so you can browse hassle free and not be bothered by anyone trying to pitch you or twisting your arm. If salespeople do approach you, tell them you have no intention of buying, and just doing research, and would prefer to look undisturbed. If they continue to hound you walk away and go to another dealership: you probably don't want to buy from a dealership that doesn't respect the customer's wishes.

Engaging the Salesperson

Be direct and to the point not wavering in your decision, on your car choice. They already think that they have a car in mind for you to take home. Let them know what you intend to buy, share with them all of your desired options, this will let the salesperson know that you are an informed buyer and know what you want. When you are direct it will be easy to win this round. The next one is not going to be so easy.

Be positive and let the salesman know that you know that he can get the items on your list and provide you with a good customer experience. You want to build rapport with the salesperson, and ensure him that you will give a positive review on your car buying experience on the car dealership customer survey. They live for good survey ratings. Some will even say that they will not get paid if the survey does not reflect a high rating or score.

Be confident. Do not falter in your confidence that you will get your car of choice. Be steadfast and know with confidence that you will be walking out of that dealership with a car if they respond correctly to your demands.

Go to the dealership on your terms and not theirs. Be patient. You should wait until certain times before you show up at a dealership. There are times that they want your business and are willing to do anything possible to close the deal for you.

Best Times To Buy A Car

- 2nd week in October
- 3rd week in December
- Raining or inclement days. If you know it is going to rain for more than 2 days you should wait to go early on the third day before the weather clears up.

Getting the best pricing

Know the value of the car you want to purchase. This is the first step to getting the best possible deal. Go on the internet, look at newspapers, watch TV ads for the car that you want and see the going sale prices. Be prepared to produce a competitor's price, rates, rebates and incentives. The Internet has made it easier than ever to find out the dealer's cost for each car and its options. Know your target price.

Get quotes from local dealerships that you are interested in. You can do this through the internet. You will most likely be very near your bottom line price when you complete this sparing exercise..

Be the person that is buying a car, not the person that is being sold a car. Let the car dealer tell his associates this certain person, which was you, came in and purchased a certain type of car for this certain amount of money. Do not let the salesman tell his coworkers that he sold this car to this person for this amount of money with this interest rate (whatever amount that he gave you without your negotiated interest rate).

Down payment is an option, not a must in order to buy a car. Only pay a down payment if you have the money to do so, this will help you get a lower monthly payment. Do not blow your lower monthly payments by accepting a high interest rate. You will still end up paying the amount of money as if you did not have a down payment.

The higher the profit for the dealership, the higher the commission that the dealer will earn. Obviously, this motivates salespeople to build profit into the deal so they can hit profit margin goals.

Do not be a buyer that is caught off guard and exploited. Do not be a person that is weak or uninformed. Dealerships encourages their salespeople to use pressure to speed up a deal, to get a customer to accept high payments, and to get the customer to buy a car they really didn't want.

Trade in

When trading in a car homework must be done here also to help your bottom line. Look at the Kelly bluebook for the trade in value of your vehicle. Ask for more like they ask for more on their cars. Request a trade in value that you would like to get for your vehicle.

Have the vehicle detailed much as possible, this will raise the rating of your trade in when they began to place a value on it and you can argue that the vehicle should be valued more until they raise the value for you. Especially when you have no damage to the body, clean interior and it runs great. Everything is negotiated, even your trade in.

Sometimes it pays to trade in a car of no value to you. By doing this you and the dealership have something to work with to make numbers adjust to suite your payment. A car that is worth 500 dollars in your opinion, can translate to 1,500 to 2,000 dollars as a trade in value that will help the bottom line.

Don't allow them to attach the trade in value of your trade-in car to the price of your new car.

Get the bottom line price on the car before introducing a trade-in. You do not want a case where the dealership has your trade in and you have a car that they supposed to have use the trade in value toward the purchase, but instead they have stolen your trade-in and you have purchased their new vehicle with no trade-in impact. The dealership on the other hand has your vehicle that they will sell and you receive no advantages from the trade in.

Trade in are a funny and tricky little item. The dealer takes your trade in and asks the used car manager how much he would give for the car. The manager says $4,000 and the salesperson tells you that the trade in value is around $2,000, so negotiate for $3,000 and tell the salesperson that you thought that your trade in was worth about $6,000. If they give you $3,000 then the salesperson received $1,000 in front end money (profit) and you get $3,000 towards the purchase of your new car. Back end profit is what's made on interest, holdbacks, and elements of the deal. If he loses this round and you get full value for your traded in car he is bound to try and take the next round, so be prepared. Just think that sometimes they are willing to lose in order to make the sale.

Do not be afraid to keep your car and go through the deal without a trade in. You could on the other hand retain your car and sell your car to another party, and have this positive cash in your pocket to do as you please with it.

Negotiating your monthly payment

State your desired monthly payment amount. They are looking for a number from you. With that in mind, do not be surprised the first number that they throw at you. Now you guys are ready for round two of about a ten round match. Be prepared to stay the distance, even if the fight goes into the next day. Hold your own. Meaning to hold on to your money. They would like to break you down inside and make you feel that if you want their beautiful and brand new car that you are going to have to pay for it.

This amount should be reasonable of course. Looking

at the price of the vehicle that you want. With months extended far out as possible. You should be looking at about $100 a month for every $5,000 of sale. So for a car with the value of about $20,000, you should be looking at the $400 range of payment. Go with the longest terms in month that are possible. By doing this your car payment will be lower than a short term arrangement. This is how you should calculate your payment and be reasonable.

They on the other hand calculate a little bit differently. They would love for every $10,000 that you financed, that the down payment they would love to get is $3,000 and the monthly payment they try for is $250. This way, a $20,000 vehicle would require you to put about $6,000 down and have a $500 a monthly payment. This payment method is based on a high interest rate calculated on five- year loans. The numbers represent inflated cost with a ridiculously high interest rate that they in the business call, really stupid high numbers.

Request 0% interest or lowest interest possible. Do not be afraid to ask for a lower rate and also be prepared to walk out because of this reason. Tell them that the interest rate is holding up the deal between you and them. That you must end this negotiation at this time. Take his card and leave. They will most likely call you back the next day and try to work out something with you. Tell them that you are looking for a stress free experience.

Request corporate incentive for price reduction. 1. A lot of cooperation have in place with dealerships for their employees to receive a reduced priced for their vehicles when they are purchased thru that program. 2. If you do not ask for this program, the dealership will not mention it unless it is to their advantage and prevent you from walking out. 3. This price is mostly and likely to be the dealer invoice price.

Finance Office

Request corporate incentive for price reduction, if you work for a major cooperation. This chance may happen in the finance office if the salesperson only job was to help you pick out your vehicle. This should happen one or two places, in the finance office or at the salesperson's desk before you get to the finance office.

Request low interest rate at this time also, if it has not been covered by the salesperson. If you have great credit, you are in the driver's seat here. Request the lowest interest possible and have them to show you where you sit at on the interest scale because of your credit score. It is a good idea to know your credit score before shopping for a new car.

When you are a first time car buyer there may be some deals that you are eligible for, so be sure that you tell the dealer that you are a first time buyer and looking for an incentive to go along with your package.

When you are in a certain profession there are deals out there for you also. For example, a teacher may get an incentive just because she is a teacher.

Car warranties are handled at this point in the finance office. At this point you must remember that anything that you do here will reflect upon your payment. Usually a $20 increase to every $900-$1000 dollars add on of any sort.

You will most likely get an extended warranty offered to you. I will step out on a limb here and say that some cars are manufactured just a little bit better than others. In my opinion Toyota, Nissan and Honda products are good enough to walk off of the lot without extended warranties. There are many products that the dealership will try to offer you. These products could tack on at least $100 – $140 onto your well negotiated car note if you allow it.

Some places will offer you a GAP warranty. That is an insurance that if you should total your car, that you will not be responsible for the remaining balance due on the car to the company. This is one of the products that I recommend getting.

Products that I can do without: tire warranty, paint warranty, anti-theft packages along with electrical warranty. Just remember that these are products, and also you came in the dealership for a car not a lot of additional products that you can do without. The finance manager isn't there just for the paperwork. He or she wants to sell you high-profit financial and mechanical add-ons. These are seldom worth the money. If the salesperson presses for an extended bumper to bumper warranty let them know the only way that you will take it is if they reduce or lower the price of the car for a few hundred dollars.

In California, and maybe some other states, there may be a no "cooling off period." A cooling off period allows for you to change your mind within a certain period of signing a contract. For example, if you decide that the car cost too much money you can cancel the contract.

2. BUYING A CAR FROM AN INDIVIDUAL

When buying a car from an individual there are many details to pay attention to as well. You still need to be prepared, like knowing your budget and utilizing the same strategies you would if you were buying a car from a car dealership.

Check the interior

Be careful and examine the car before you buy it and look for:

- Stained interior, carpets
- Ripped material
- Cracked leather on the seats, arm rest and dashboard
- Interior lights that are burned out
- Electronics i.e. radio, CD player, USB or input jacks
- Cigarette lighter and dc output plugs
- Light lens covers that may be cracked or broken

- Mirrors

Check the exterior

- Doors, trunk and hood open and close okay
- Light lens covers that may be cracked or broken
- Tail lights, head light and license plate light
- Hail damage on the body
- Repainted areas (look for overspray on the rubber molding)
- Black smoke from the tail pipe
- Broken, cracked or nicked windshield
- Worn or uneven tire wear. Uneven wear in the front could mean the wheels or suspension are out of alignment
- Look under the car for rust. It could be expensive to replace a frame

Mechanical (under the hood)

- Look for oil spots on the ground
- Check oil level before the engine is cranked and check the color of the oil to see if it looks burnt or dark black and if it is easy to drip off of the dipstick (it should not be thin)
- Fluids leaking from the car
- With the hood open, look for missing covers and caps and check the spark plugs if possible to see if they are newer than the car. This may indicate that the car has had a tune up or has undergone regular maintenance.
- Look for steam that may be coming from the engine after running for a while.
- Black smoke from the tail pipe
- Check inside gauges for rising temperature and high oil pressure.
- Check to see if any service lights are on (engine,

oil, tire, etc)
- Check mirrors operation switch and seat switches

Test driving the used car

Always be sure that you test drive the car that you are buying new or used. The new car dealer will try to get you in it to test drive. They are very confident that the feel of the wheel will seal the deal. See it as a red flag if the used car seller does not want you to test drive the car.

Have the engine cranked and let it run for a while to allow the engine to heat up.

Observe if you have to turn the key a lot to get the car started. If so, there may be a problem in the ignition system of the car.

Listen to the engine to hear any knocks.

Observe if the car shakes when accelerating and decelerating. See if the motor raises up on one side and the rpms are increase. This may indicate loose or worn engine mount problems.

Maneuver tight turns and full right and left turns to have the steering turned all the way to the right and left and check for popping noises. This will check the ball joints.

Do not just test drive on the local streets. Take the vehicle out on the freeway also to see if you like it's acceleration, braking, cabin sound, feel of the seats, cruise control, tilted steering, audio and visual system if available and anything else that you can observe.

Observe how the car shift to another gear. It should not make a clunking noise or hesitate when switching gears. You should not hear grinding noise when shifting manually. Also, check the clutch of a manual transmission by going slowly uphill in a higher than normal gear, like 3rd or 4th gear. If the clutch is good, the RPM will decrease and nearly stall. If the clutch is bad, the engine will rev but won't go anywhere.

Check the brakes when test driving by accelerating to about 50 mph. Depress the brakes hard. Check to see if the car pulls to one side or another, it may mean you have a loose brake caliper or there's not enough hydraulic fluid. Also, if you feel a shuddering when you brake, it could mean the brakes are warped. The brake pedal should also feel firm when you depress the brakes.. If the brake sinks all the way to the floor, you should not be driving this car. There may be a need to replace the master cylinder. I once did not take this serious by not replacing the master cylinder and it finally gave out on me and I could not pump enough vacuum back into the lines before I entered into an intersection and had a wreck. Which I was entirely at fault.

Legal

When buying a car from an individual you should pay close attention to the legal aspect of the transaction.

Make sure the the title belongs to the person that you are buying the car from

Look at the odometer reading to see if it average out to approximately 15-17 thousand miles per year in correlation with the year it was manufactured.

If the car indicate it has low miles but the wear and tear on the inside looks like it's been to a jungle and back something might be suspicious.

Look for a valid inspection sticker date (if your state requires cars to be inspected).

When was the last time the car has been registered? If over a year, ask why it was not registered. If the car has not be registered for an extended length of time you will have to pay for the years that it was not registered to bring the registration up to date.

Ask how many owners has there been, if the car has ever been in an accident, what type of mechanical problems were there, if any, and the maintenance history of the vehicle.

You will have to transfer the title into your name at the Department of Motor Vehicles. You will need a Bill of Sales from the buyer with the purchase price, VIN #, you and the buyer signature alone with the date and proof of insurance.

3. BUYING A CAR AT AN AUCTION

Buying a car at an auction is another way of obtaining a car that many people do not consider. Just like the other ways of buying a car you still must be diligent in this process also.

Arrive early enough to look at the cars ahead of time before the auction began. This will allow you eliminate cars that you will not be bidding on. Also this will allow you ample amount of time to really look at the cars that are up for auction.

Becoming a bidder

There is usually an entry fee of about $200. This money will entitle you to have a bidding number. You will be refunded this money if you do not win a bid on a car. In the event that you win a bid the entry fee will be applied to the purchase of the car.

Actual Auction

When you hold up your number, paddle, or hand, you have said to the auctioneer that you have accepted that bid number amount. There will be other people bidding as well. If you are the last one to bid without anyone else bidding you win the bid and the amount that was last announced by the auctioneer.

They will make a note of your number. Most likely write it on the windshield of the car along with the last bid amount and proceed to move that vehicle out of the way for another vehicle to be auctioned. The vehicles may just be stationary and the auctioneer will move on to the next vehicle in line to be auctioned off.

Take note of the crowd and do not get into a bidding war with a car dealer or a car dealer representative. They have come with money and are experienced at bidding on cars. For example, some dealers will run up a bid on a car and then drop out of the bidding war for that particular car in order to eliminate bidding competition from other cars. By running up bids they allow for themselves to be the only ones with a budget left for other desirable cars.

Title Transfer

When you are finished bidding and have won the bid or bids, you may proceed to pay for the vehicle or stay and bid on other cars. Let me stress that if you bid on 5 cars and win all 5 you are held responsible for paying for all of the cars. You will not be able to get to the window and decide to pick what car or cars you would like to purchase out of those that you won the bids for.

For those who may have a means to fix cars or have a means to tow cars sometime at the end of auctions that location may have some cars that they will take as little as $100 or less, just to move them off of the lot. You can then decide if you would like to repair, fix, or junk these cars to make money or to sell.

Just like you would from a dealership you will be issued a temporary tag once you have purchased the car. Your car plates shall arrive at the location where you purchased your vehicle to pick up.

4. WOMEN BUYERS

Most car salespeople are males. Some salesmen will attempt to take advantage of females who are buying alone, they will think that the female is not concerned about all the aspects that goes into buying car. I am not saying that females can't and shouldn't buy cars alone, however bringing a male figure along to the car dealership is a good idea.

This male figure does not have to make any deals for you. He may be just there to give you some heads up on some things that he has insight on. Remember that, even if he says nothing, he has just leveled the field and placed a little balance in your favor.

Some salesmen will try to distract you with their charm but they still have their own interest and agenda in mind. Men are less likely to try to pull something over a woman's head when there is a male present.

Car salespeople are usually males and for some reason men feel like they can just tell a woman anything and they will believe it.

Salesmen will often make themselves seem like an authoritative figure, use intimidation, or sell a female a car instead of allow her to buy the car of her choice. I have seen this happen many times.

As a woman it is important to not keep silent, and not be afraid to negotiate for exactly what you want out of the deal. If you want a sunroof, rims, spoiler, a lower interest rate, or any other option make sure to leave with everything and that you are happy with your car purchase.

Don't feel pressured into signing a contract. Listen to your intuition and don't be afraid to walk away from the car dealership if you feel uncomfortable about the sales tactics or the deal being offered.

5. SUCCESSFUL AND NOT SO SUCCESSFUL PURCHASES

Vehicle #1.

My daughter thought that she could go on her own without me or her brother, uncle or a male figure. Very confident in what she does. She still was not able to overcome that maleness, that sharpness, that keen, over zealousness of the male salesman. The vehicle does looks good, I will grant her that, but in the long run of things. It was overpriced, he stole her trade-in. She still managed to get out without a down payment. She does not have any extras more than what comes out of the factory. Plus she went to a Hyundai dealership which I think are overpriced stylish vehicles. She was sold a gray car, not one with color, no chrome anywhere on the body. Well the story goes on and on and on............

Vehicle # 2

Vehicle # 2 was good deal. I purchased this one for my wife. I advised her to search on the internet, the price, the color, the options that she wanted. I used all of the tactics that I mentioned above and she was very satisfied with the vehicle. Her next vehicle was a Honda CRV, a model of the next year before they hit the street. Another great purchase and she loves it with all of the options available that can come on it plus some aftermarket items also.

Vehicle # 3

Vehicle # 3 is the Lincoln Navigator which is on the cover page of this article. I purchased this great fine at an auction for only $2,500. This has a Kelly Blue Book value of over $4,500. Nice vehicle using my methods describe in the article. Sold for $5,150.

Vehicle # 4

The next vehicle is examples #4, The Gold Chevrolet Equinox. See it does not matter where you go to get a vehicle. It can even be a motorcycle dealership. The principle works with them all. Everyone is trying to look out for their money. The person that is not or is caught unaware is going to be the loser. So in this case, I want the dealership to be unaware that I have the information that I have. Remember that information changes the situation. A great vehicle that could have been used to overcharge me. By using the tools that I had knowledge of, I was once again the winner.

Vehicle # 5

This plan also works when purchasing vehicles from rental car places such as my next example, vehicle #5 which is the white PT Cruiser, which was not included in my article, because the location where you are getting the vehicles matters not one bit.

Vehicle # 6

    This is a 2014 Honda CRV purchased in 2013. This is the vehicle that I asked my wife to build with all of the options that she could think of even the aftermarket options that she wanted to see, just to prove to her my techniques work across the board. My wife came out on top with a car that she just loves, as she puts it. "I just love my car and thank you so much for it". I was happy that she wanted it in black. After seeing how that black PT Cruiser look. I wanted us to soon have matching color cars.

Vehicle # 7

This is example number 7, a Nissan Altima SL edition. This vehicle I purchased too early because the 2014 editions were not yet manufactured and had not come off of the assembly line. I little homework that I missed, not knowing exactly when the 2014 cars were available for sale to individuals. But I am satisfied with my purchased. This car is an SL edition that I upgraded with options that made it look like an SV edition. The SV is the top package in Nissan vehicles. Like the spoiler, sunroof and additional fog lights which comes standard on the SV editions which cost substantially more that the SL edition.

CONCLUSION

This concludes my thought and ideals on the subject of how to buy a car. There may be up date from time to time. But for right now, I think that you will be able to come out a winner and feel good about what you have purchased and not what they have sold you. Best Wishes and Endeavors to You!

DISCLAIMER

I assume no liability for any actions that you take or do during your negotiation of the purchase of a vehicle. All risk incidental or otherwise, arising from the use or misunderstanding of this information contained herein ar entirely the responsibility of the reader and users of this information. Although careful precaution has been taken in the preparation of this material, I assume no responsibility for omissions or errors or assumptions, whether such assumptions, errors or omissions result from negligence, accidents or any other cause. No part of this publication may be reproduced, stored in a retrieval system or transmitted in any form or by any means nor be circulated in any form of binding or cover other than which it is published and without a similar condition without a similar condition including this condition being imposed on the subsequent purchaser without the prior permission in writing. You shall pursue no judgments toward me or anyone else concerning this material. You shall in no means use this material in a court of law for no reason. You may not duplicate, reprint or copy any parts or portions of this document for any purpose.

ABOUT THE AUTHOR

I was born in Memphis, TN. in the early fifties. My first car I purchased was from an individual and it was a 1959 Chevrolet for $100.00 in 1971. Since then I have been around the world, obtained an international driver license and have purchased vehicles overseas also. I have purchased cars from auctions, individuals, used and new car dealerships, car rental outlets and anywhere else a person can buy a vehicle. I wrote a short book, How to Win at Auctions, and have advised people all over as what to say and do when buying their first car. I live in Dallas, Texas the home of trucks and big cars. I am dedicated to helping any and every one that I can to get a good deal when purchasing their vehicles. Contact the author at devoep@gmail.com.